VOLCANOES

SEYMOUR SIMON

PICTURE CREDITS
National Park Service, Hawaii Volcanoes National Park, pages 7, 19, 26;
Gary Rosenquist/Earth Images, page 11;
Seymour Simon, pages 24, 25, 32;
Solarfilma, pages 15, 16, 17;
Terraphotographics/BPS, pages 8, 9, 12 (B. J. O'Donnel), 13 (both), 27
(John K. Nakata),
28, 29, 30 (Carl May), 31;
U.S. Geological Survey, J. D. Griggs, pages 4, 20, 21, 23.

Printed in Singapore. For information address HarperCollins
Children's Books, a division of HarperCollins Publishers,
1350 Avenue of the Americas, New York, NY 10019.
www.harperchildrens.com
7   8   9   10
Library of Congress Cataloging-in-Publication Data
Simon, Seymour.
Volcanoes / Seymour Simon.
p.   cm.
Summary: Explains, in simple terms, the characteristics of
volcanoes and describes some famous eruptions and their aftermath.
ISBN 0-688-07411-1 (trade) — ISBN 0-688-07412-X (lib. bdg.)
ISBN 0-688-14029-7 (pbk.)
1. Volcanoes—Juvenile literature.   [1. Volcanoes.]   I. Title.
QE521.3.S56   1988
551.2'1—dc19   87-33316   CIP   AC

To my sister
Miriam Simon Beyman

hroughout history, people have told stories about volcanoes. The early Romans believed in Vulcan, their god of fire. They thought that Vulcan worked at a hot forge, striking sparks as he made swords and armor for the other gods. It is from the Roman god Vulcan that we get the word *volcano.*

The early Hawaiians told legends of the wanderings of Pele, their goddess of fire. Pele was chased from her homes by her sister Namaka, goddess of the sea. Pele moved constantly from one Hawaiian island to another. Finally, Pele settled in a mountain called Kilauea, on the big island of Hawaii. Even though the islanders tried to please Pele, she burst forth every few years. Kilauea is still an active volcano.

n early times, no one knew how volcanoes formed or why they spouted fire. In modern times, scientists began to study volcanoes. They still don't know all the answers, but they know much about how a volcano works.

Our planet is made up of many layers of rock. The top layers of solid rock are called the crust. Deep beneath the crust, it is so hot that some rock melts. The melted, or molten, rock is called magma.

Volcanoes are formed by cracks or holes that poke through the earth's crust. Magma pushes its way up through the cracks. This is called a volcanic eruption. When magma pours forth on the surface it is called lava. In this photograph of an eruption, you can see great fountains of boiling lava forming fiery rivers and lakes. As lava cools, it hardens to form rock.

A volcano can be two things: a hole in the ground that lava comes through, or a hill or mountain formed by the lava. Mount Rainier in the state of Washington is a volcano even though it has not erupted since 1882.

Not far from Mount Rainier (top, right) is Mount St. Helens (bottom, left). Native Americans and early settlers in the Northwest had seen Mount St. Helens puff out some ashes, steam, and lava in the mid-1800s. Yet for more than a century, the mountain seemed quiet and peaceful.

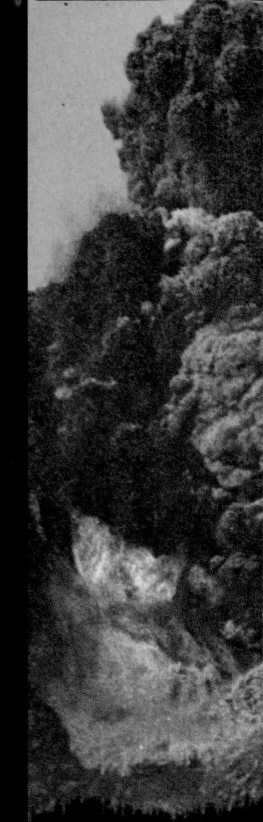

n March 1980 Mount St. Helens awakened from its long sleep. First there were a few small earthquakes that shook the mountain. Then on March 27 Mount St. Helens began to spout ashes and steam. Each day brought further quakes, until by mid-May more than ten thousand small quakes had been recorded. The mountain began to swell up and crack.

Sunday May 18 dawned bright and clear. The mountain seemed much the same as it had been for the past month. Suddenly, at 8:32 A.M., Mount St. Helens erupted with incredible force. The energy released in the eruption was equal to ten million tons of dynamite.

The eruption of Mount St. Helens was the most destructive in the history of the United States. Sixty people lost their lives as hot gases, rocks, and ashes covered an area of two hundred thirty square miles. Hundreds of houses and cabins were destroyed, leaving many people homeless. Miles of highways, roads, and railways were badly damaged. The force of the eruption was so great that entire forests were blown down like rows of matchsticks.

Compare the way Mount St. Helens looked before and after the eruption. The entire top of the mountain was blown away. In its place is a huge volcanic crater. In 1982 the mountain and the area around it were dedicated as the Mount St. Helens National Volcanic Monument. Visitor centers allow people to view the volcano's astonishing power.

Volcanoes don't just happen anyplace. The earth's crust is broken into huge sections like a giant cracked eggshell. The pieces of the crust are called plates. The United States, Canada, and Mexico and part of the North Atlantic Ocean are all on the North American plate. Almost all the volcanoes in the world erupt in places where two plates meet.

Down the middle of the North Atlantic Ocean, two plates are slowly moving apart. Hot magma pushes up

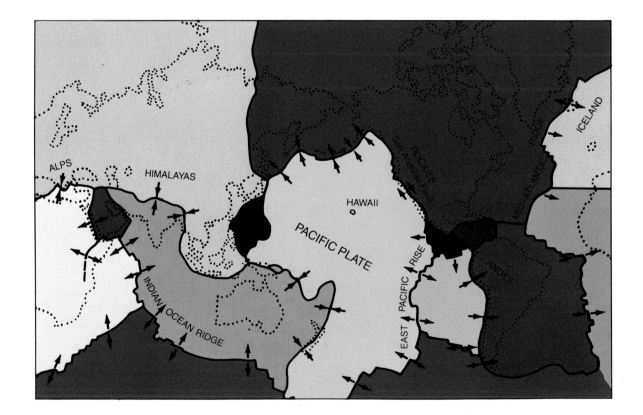

between them. A chain of underwater volcanoes runs along the line where the two plates meet. Some of the underwater volcanoes have grown so high that they stick up from the ocean floor to make islands.

Iceland is a volcanic island in the North Atlantic. In 1963, an area of the sea near Iceland began to smoke. An undersea volcano was exploding and a new island was being formed. The island was named Surtsey, after the ancient Norse god of fire.

Ten years after the explosion that formed Surtsey, another volcano erupted near Iceland. It was off the south coast of Iceland on the island of Heimaey. Within six hours of the eruption, more than 5,000 people were taken off the island to safety. After two months, hundreds of buildings had burned down and dozens more had been buried in the advancing lava. Then the volcano stopped erupting. After a year's time, the people of Heimaey came back to reclaim their island with its new 735-foot volcano.

ost volcanoes and earthquakes are along the edges of the large Pacific plate. There are so many that the shoreline of the Pacific Ocean is called the "Ring of Fire." But a few volcanoes are not on the edge of a plate. The volcanoes in the Hawaiian Islands are in the middle of the Pacific plate.

A million years ago, magma pushed up through cracks in the Pacific plate. Over the years, eruption followed eruption. Little by little, thin layers of lava hardened, one atop another. Thousands of eruptions were needed to build mountains high enough to reach from the deep sea bottom and appear as islands.

The largest Hawaiian volcano is Mauna Loa. It is seventy miles long and rises thirty thousand feet from the ocean floor. It is still growing. Every few years, Mauna Loa erupts again.

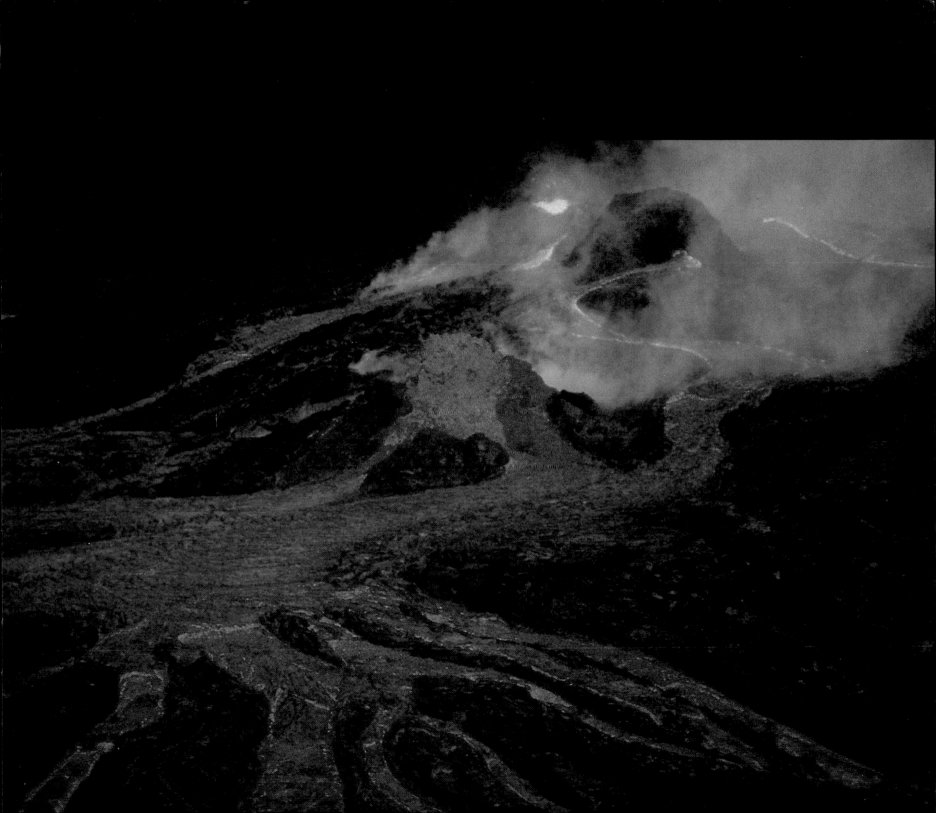

Hawaiian volcano lava usually bubbles out quietly to form rivers or lakes, or spouts a few hundred feet in the air in a fiery fountain. Hawaiian volcanoes erupt much more gently than did Surtsey or Mount St. Helens. Only rarely does a Hawaiian volcano throw out rock and high clouds of ash.

Steam clouds billow as a flow of hot lava enters the sea. Hawaii is constantly changing as eruptions add hundreds of acres of new land to the islands. In other parts of the shoreline, old lava flows are quickly weathered by the waves into rocks and black sand.

awaiian lava is thin and flows quickly. In some lava rivers, speeds as high as thirty-five miles per hour have been measured. In an eruption in 1986, a number of houses were threatened by the quick-moving lava. Fire fighters sprayed water on the lava to slow down its advance.

When lava cools and hardens, it forms volcanic rocks. The kinds of rocks formed are clues to the kind of eruption. The two main kinds have Hawaiian names. Thick, slow-moving lava called *aa* (AH-ah)

hardens into a rough tangle of sharp rocks. Thin, hot, quick-moving lava called *pahoehoe* (pah-HO-ee-ho-ee) forms a smooth, billowy surface.

Earth scientists have divided volcanoes into four groups. Shield volcanoes, such as Mauna Loa and Kilauea, have broad, gentle slopes shaped like an ancient warrior's shield.

Cinder cone volcanoes look like upside-down ice cream cones. They erupt explosively, blowing out burning ashes and cinders. The ashes and cinders build up to form the cone shape. The cinder cone volcano to the near left erupted in Guatemala, Central America, in 1984. The cinder cone volcanoes in the background are still smoking from earlier eruptions.

Most of the volcanoes in the world are composite or strato-volcanoes. Strato-volcanoes are formed by the lava, cinders, and ashes of an eruption. During an eruption, ashes and cinders fall to the ground. The eruption quiets down and lava slowly flows out, covering the layer of ashes and cinders. Further eruptions add more layers of ashes and cinders, followed by more layers of lava. Mount Shasta (above) in California and Mount Hood (below) in Oregon are strato-volcanoes. They are still active even though they have not erupted for many years.

The fourth kind of volcano is called a dome volcano. Dome volcanoes have thick, slow-moving lava that forms a steep-sided dome shape. After an eruption, the volcano may be plugged with hardened lava. The plug prevents the gases from escaping, like a cork in a bottle of soda water. As the pressure builds up, the volcano blows its top, as Mount St. Helens did. Lassen Peak in California is a dome volcano that erupted violently in 1915. You can see the huge chunks of volcanic rock near the summit.

Around the world there are many very old volcanoes that no longer erupt. These dead volcanoes are called extinct. Crater Lake in Oregon is an extinct volcano. Almost seven thousand years ago, Mount Mazama in Oregon erupted, sending out a thick blanket of ashes that covered the ground for miles around. Then the entire top of the volcano collapsed. A huge crater, called a caldera, formed and was later filled with water. Crater Lake reaches a depth of two thousand feet, the deepest lake in North America.

After a volcano erupts, everything is buried under lava or ashes. Plants and animals are nowhere to be found. But in a few short months, life renews itself. Plants grow in the cracks between the rocks. Insects and other animals return. Volcanoes do not just destroy. They bring new mountains, new islands, and new soil to the land. Many good things can come from the fiery explosions of volcanoes.